IOWA

in words and pictures

BY DENNIS B. FRADIN

ILLUSTRATIONS BY RICHARD WAHL

MAPS BY LEN W. MEENTS

Consultant
 Dr. Donald A. Scovel
 Professor, Social Studies Education
 Price Laboratory School
 University of Northern Iowa
 Cedar Falls, Iowa

CHILDRENS PRESS ®

CHICAGO

To Clarence and Mabel Hill of Minburn, Iowa

Effigy Mounds National Monument at the Mississippi River

Library of Congress Cataloging in Publication Data

Fradin, Dennis B.
  Iowa in words and pictures.

  SUMMARY: An introduction to the state named after
the Ioway Indians.
  1. Iowa—Juvenile literature. [1. Iowa]
I. Wahl, Richard, 1939- II. Meents, Len W.
III. Title.
F621.3.F72   977.7   79-19399
ISBN 0-516-03915-6

Picture Acknowledgments:
JAMES P. ROWAN—cover, 2, 11, 23, 43
IOWA DEVELOPMENT COMMISSION—5, 15, 26, 27, 28, 30, 33(right)
DUBUQUE AREA CHAMBER OF COMMERCE—8, 36
GREATER DES MOINES CHAMBER OF COMMERCE FEDERATION—17,
22, 31, 32, 33(left), 42
TOM WINTER—34
COVER PHOTO—Iowa farmland

7 8 9 10 11 R 93 92 91 90 89 88

Iowa (I • o • ah) was named after the Ioway Indians, who once roamed the land. Iowa is one of America's great farming states. It is famous for corn and hogs.

But Iowa has much more than hogs and corn. It has lovely rolling hills. It has rivers and streams. It also has cities where tractors and washing machines are made.

Do you know where Indians built dirt mounds shaped like people and animals? Do you know which state has the highest percentage of people who can read and write? Do you know where President Hoover, "Buffalo Bill" Cody, and John Wayne were born? Do you know which state has the *most* farmers?

As you will learn, the answer to these questions is—
Iowa.

Over a million years ago, the Ice Age began.
Mountains of ice called *glaciers* (GLAY • shurs) covered
Iowa. Glaciers flattened the land. They ground up hills
into good rich soil. Thanks to glaciers, Iowa was left with
great farm land.

Indians called *Mound Builders* came to Iowa
thousands of years ago. They built over 10,000 mounds in
Iowa. Small mounds were used to bury the dead.
Skeletons have been found inside. The Mound Builders
used wooden bows and arrows. They made farm tools out
of stone. They grew corn and other crops.

Prehistoric Indian mounds were built in the shape of animals.

Some mounds these ancient (AIN • chent) people made were *very* big. In Iowa there are mounds shaped like birds, bears, wolves, and snakes. There is even one shaped like a giant woman. Why were these big mounds built? No one knows. Scientists are digging in Iowa and other places to learn more about the Mound Builders.

In recent times, a number of Indian tribes lived in Iowa. Indians in Iowa grew corn, pumpkins, potatoes, and melons. They hunted deer and buffalo with bows and arrows. They made their clothes of deerskin. Indians often planted corn in the spring, hunted all summer, then returned home to harvest the corn in the fall. Indians who traveled a lot carried tents, called *tepees*. Indians who stayed in one place built houses of tree bark.

Some of the tribes in Iowa were the Ioway, Oto (OD • oh), Missouri (mih • ZOOR • ee), Illinois (ILL • ah • noy), Ottawa (OTT • ah • wah), Sioux (SUE), Sauk (SAWK), Fox, and Mascoutins (ma • SKOOT • ins). These tribes did not always get along. They fought wars over the land.

The French were the first outsiders to explore Iowa. In the summer of 1673 Father Marquette (mar • KETT) and Louis Joliet (LOU • ee JOE • lee • ett) traveled by canoe down the Mississippi River. On June 25, Joliet and Marquette came to shore near the present town of

Oakville. They saw some footprints. They followed the
footprints to an Indian village. The explorers and the
Indians looked each other over. Both the Frenchmen and
the Indians made signs of peace.

More Frenchmen explored Iowa. In 1680 Father
Hennepin (HEN • a • pin) explored the Iowa shore of the
Mississippi River. In 1682 the explorer La Salle claimed
a huge area, which included Iowa, for France.

A few French fur traders came to Iowa. They traded blankets and knives to the Indians. In return they received animal skins which could be made into clothes. The Frenchman Julien Dubuque (ZHU • lean da • BUKE) was the first settler in Iowa. Lead—used to make bullets—was found along the Mississippi River. In 1788 the Fox Indians let Dubuque mine the lead. Dubuque learned the Indians' language. He traded with them. He farmed.

The town that grew near Dubuque's lead mine was named after Dubuque.

Dubuque, with the Mississippi River in the background

In 1799 the Frenchman Louis Honore Tesson (o • nor • RAY tay • SON) rode by mule into southeast Iowa. He started a farm. He grew potatoes and corn. He also brought some baby apple trees with him. Those baby apple trees grew into Iowa's *first* apple orchard.

In 1803 France sold a large piece of land, including Iowa, to the United States. Iowa wasn't a state yet. It was a territory. Until it became a state 43 years later, Iowa was part of different territories, including the Iowa Territory. In 1804 Meriwether Lewis (MAR • i • WEH • ther LOU • iss) and William Clark explored Iowa along the Missouri River for the United States.

Men from the American Fur Company set up a number of trading posts in Iowa. Towns like Council Bluffs, Sioux City, Muscatine (muss • KAH • teen), Eddyville, Keokuk (KEY • ah • kuck), and Davenport grew up where the men traded furs with the Indians.

Iowa had room for both the pioneers and the Indians. At first, many Indians were friendly to the pioneers. But then many Indians became angry when they saw that the U.S. government wanted them off the land. The Indians were sometimes given liquor. Then they were forced to sign treaties giving up their land. Some Indians just left Iowa and went farther west. Others fought. Black Hawk, chief of the Sauk tribe, was angry that Indians were being pushed farther and farther west.

In 1832, Black Hawk led a band of Sauk and Fox Indians against the white soldiers. The fighting was mainly in Wisconsin (wis • KAHN • sin) and Illinois. Black Hawk lost what came to be known as the Black Hawk War. Black Hawk gave up his Iowa lands. After that, other Indians made a series of treaties giving up their lands. The Sauk, the Fox, and the Sioux gave up all their Iowa lands. Only a few Sauk and Fox Indians were allowed to stay on a small reservation in Tama County.

However, as late as 1857 some Sioux killed 42 settlers in the Spirit Lake Massacre (MASS • ah • kur), in Iowa.

After the Black Hawk War the news spread across America: "There's great farmland in Iowa!" Whole families headed towards Iowa. Most came by covered wagons, pulled by oxen. Lots of families often came together, making a "wagon train." They carried everything they owned with them: cows, pigs, sheep, farm tools, and furniture. There were no good roads

Iowa farmland

then. People followed Indian trails where they could.
Sometimes friendly Indians showed them streams where
they could get water. The travelers shot birds and deer
for food. They crossed the Mississippi River by putting
their wagons on huge flatboats. Once across the
Mississippi, they were in Iowa. They were pioneers—
new people in the area.

The pioneers usually built their homes near streams, so
they would have drinking water. Some pioneers made
"dugout homes." They dug out the side of a hill. Then

they covered it with branches for a roof. Other pioneers made "sod houses." They cut the sod—prairie grass mixed with dirt—into brick-sized pieces. The sod bricks were used to make the walls. The roof of the "soddy" was made with branches covered by more sod.

"Dugout homes" and "sod houses" were good-looking houses when well made. And what did they cost to build? Nothing—just a lot of hard work.

Where there were trees, some pioneers made log cabins. The windows were covered with animal skins instead of glass. Often the floor was just the earth.

The pioneers used skunk fat to light their lamps. The Iowa settlers helped each other. When a new family arrived, the older pioneers helped them build their house.

The pioneers had come to farm. They raised milk cows, pigs, and sheep. Planting was hard. The sod was tough. It was hard to break it up with wooden plows. Some early Iowa farmers just took their hoes and chopped up the sod. Then they dropped the seeds into the earth, and hoped that the crops would grow.

And did they grow! Corn grew so well in Iowa that even the farmers were surprised. That great soil, left by glaciers, helped it grow so well. After they harvested the corn the farmers ground it up. Animals and people ate the corn. Iowa farmers also grew wheat and oats.

Today, farmers use modern machinery to plant corn.

Field corn ready to be harvested.

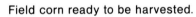

15

By 1840, 43,000 settlers lived in Iowa. By 1846 over a hundred thousand people had come to Iowa, most of them because of the great farmland. Iowa became our 29th state on December 28, 1846. The first capital of the new state was Iowa City. Iowa became known as the *Hawkeye State*—probably because of Chief Black Hawk.

In 1848 the first telegraph was built in Iowa. Now people could send messages. In 1855 the first railroad was built. In 1856 a bridge was completed over the Mississippi River. Trains could now cross the Mississippi River and bring people to Iowa. People—mostly farmers—poured into the state.

Where many farmers lived in one area, new towns grew. Keokuk, Muscatine, Okoboji (o • kah • BO • gee), Sioux City, and Sac City were given Indian names. Marquette, Le Claire, and Dubuque were given French

names. Each town had a general store. There, farm
families could buy items sent from the east.

In the 1850s and 1860s Des Moines (deh • MOIN), Cedar
Rapids, and Waterloo grew into cities. In the cities,
business grew. But farming continued to be the lifeblood
of Iowa.

At Living History Farms, near Des Moines, visitors can learn about
farm life in Iowa before 1900.

Many of the activities of the Iowa farmers centered around corn. Taking the husks off the corn was a dull job. Iowans made it more fun by having corn-husking contests in the fall. The one who could shuck the most corn would win a prize.

Corn needs water. Without water, corn will dry up and die. During a dry summer, some early Iowa farmers would get together and hire a "rainmaker." This was a person who was supposed to be able to make it rain. If it rained, the people would pay the rainmaker $100 or more. If it didn't rain, he might be run out of town.

During the Civil War (1861-1865) the Northern states fought the Southern states. Slavery was one of the big issues during the Civil War. There were black slaves in the South. People in Iowa did not have slaves. In fact, some Iowa people helped slaves escape from the South all the way to Canada. Iowa fought on the side of the North during the Civil War. Farmers left their homes and joined the army. Iowans fought in Civil War battles at Vicksburg, Shiloh (SHY • low), and Atlanta. One group of Iowa soldiers, the "Greybeards," were men at least forty-five years old. Some were over seventy. They helped guard Southern prisoners. Some of the Greybeards had grandchildren fighting in the army. The Greybeards and other Iowa soldiers helped the North win the Civil War.

After the Civil War the big cities of Des Moines and Cedar Rapids continued to grow. Factories began packing food products. Banking and life insurance also became big businesses in Iowa cities. But farming continued as the main source of income for Iowans. Every year farming became more scientific. Machines known as "tractors" were invented by Charles Hart and Charles Parr, of Charles City, Iowa, in about 1900. Tractors helped farmers pull their farm machines. In the early 1900s farmers did "contour planting." They

planted their crops in curved rows. This helps keep the soil from washing away during heavy rain. They also started "crop rotation." The same crop growing year after year on the same land takes minerals out of the soil. By changing—or rotating—crops, those minerals are replaced. In the 1920s a new kind of corn was developed. If two good kinds of corn are bred, you can get an even better kind of corn. This is called "hybrid (HI • bread) corn." At Iowa State College in Ames, farm experts worked on ways for farmers to have bigger and better crops. Farming had become a science.

But farming was a risky business. Weather, low prices, and high cost of land made it hard to make money. Many farmers went broke. They lost their farms. Like other businessmen, farmers learned that they had to do everything they could to make a living. In the 1930s farmers began helping themselves by joining together in groups. In these groups farmers bought seeds and other supplies together. Supplies cost less that way. They also sold their crops together, to get the most profits. These groups are called "farm cooperatives." They exist in many Iowa towns today.

In the 1940s and 1950s Iowa farmers raised so much corn and so many hogs that Iowa became known as the *Corn-Hog State.* Today, Iowa has more farm people— half a million—than any other state.

A farmers' market

Farms can be seen everywhere in Iowa.

You have learned about some of Iowa's history. Now it
is time to take a trip—in words and pictures— through
the Hawkeye State.

Iowa is near the middle of the United States. It is in the
grassy prairie region. Its land is mostly flat. But it does
have many hills. Near the rivers there are many cliffs—
called *bluffs*.

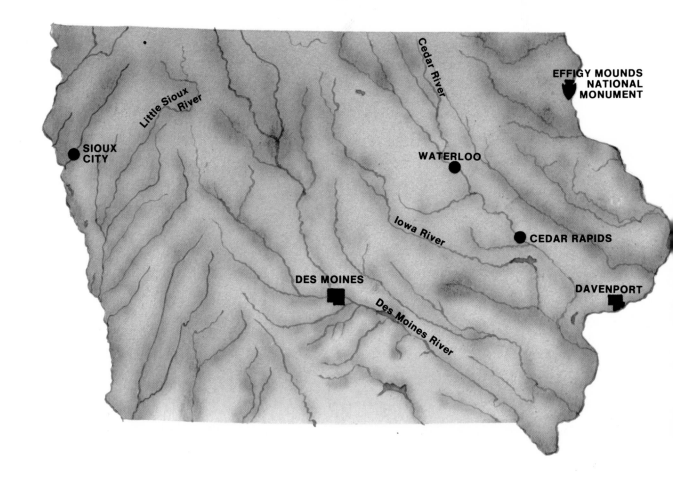

Iowa is 324 miles in its greatest distance from east to west. It is 210 miles in its greatest distance from north to south. The winding Mississippi River forms the boundary to the east. The Missouri River and the Big Sioux are on the west. Iowa is shaped like a rectangle— except where these rivers wind along the borders.

Nearly everywhere you travel in Iowa you'll see farms. The white farm houses look lovely in the clear Iowa air. You'll see red barns. You'll see green and yellow fields of corn and soybeans. You'll see cattle and horses grazing in the pastures. You'll see pigs in the hog houses. The air (except maybe near the pigs) is full of the sweetness of growing things.

You know what Iowa's leading farm crop is, of course: corn. One of Iowa's nicknames is "The Land Where the Tall Corn Grows." Corn stalks in Iowa have grown over 30 feet high. That's as high as a three-story building!

Popcorn is also grown in Iowa. Other crops grown in Iowa include soybeans, oats, hay, tomatoes, and apples. In 1881 a man named Jesse Hiatt developed a new kind of apple in Iowa. It tasted great. It was named the Delicious apple. Today, Delicious apples are eaten all over the world.

Harvesting corn

It would be interesting to visit an Iowa farm. Farmers still have to work hard. But machines make farm work easier today.

Farmers use the best corn seeds that scientists can create. Better seeds mean more corn and better corn. A corn planting machine, pulled by the farmer in his tractor, plants the seeds. Corn-picking machines pick the corn. Remember those corn-husking contests Iowans used to have? Today, machines do that, too. Sweet corn is grown for people to eat. Feed corn is grown for the farm animals to eat.

Iowa raises more hogs (pigs) than any other state. The hogs are born in clean farrowing pens. In these pens the hogs are kept warm with heat lamps. Later, the hogs are moved into hog houses. Water systems keep the hog houses clean. The hogs are fattened with feed corn. The farmers give the hogs vitamins they need to stay healthy. If one hog gets sick, the farmer calls the vet right away. One of the worst things that can happen on the farm is an outbreak of illness among the livestock. When the hogs weigh about 200 pounds, usually in the fall, they are brought to market. Hogs are made into ham, bacon, pork chops, and sausage.

Hogs

Iowa has many dairy farms. The cows on these farms give milk for people to drink. Years ago, the cows were milked by hand. Today, electric milking machines do the job. And machines kill any germs that might be in the milk, too.

Iowa farmers also raise beef cattle. The farmers fatten the cattle until they weigh 1000 pounds or more. The farmers then sell the cattle. The cattle are turned into steaks, hamburgers, and roasts for your dinner.

Cattle going to market.

Farmers have to do a lot of brain work. They have to learn about seeds. They have to learn about animals. They have to learn about weather. And they have to learn about soil. One mistake, and a whole year's crop can be ruined.

Farm people help make Iowa the "smartest" of the 50 states. Since 1910 Iowa has had a greater percentage of its people who know how to read and write than any other state. Farm people often love to read. They live by themselves. A movie show might be 30 miles away. Neighbors might be miles away, too. So farm people learned the value of reading as a source of fun as well as a necessity of life.

Farm people make many things for themselves that city people buy. They "put up"—or can—fruits and vegetables in jars. Then they have them to eat in the winter. Some farmers butcher their own hogs and cattle. Many farm women sew their own clothes, and make their own quilts, as the pioneers did.

Iowa doesn't have any really giant cities, like Chicago or New York. Even when you're in an Iowa city, you're aware that Iowa is a farming state. Trucks and trains bring farm goods into the cities. The foods are then packaged and sent all across the United States. Another nice thing about Iowa's cities is—even when you're downtown—you can drive a few miles and be out in the country.

Des Moines is Iowa's biggest city. It is the capital of Iowa. Des Moines is not far from the center of the state. It lies where the Des Moines and the Raccoon rivers meet.

A covered
bridge in
Winterset

Downtown Des Moines

Long, long ago the Mound Builders made mounds in
the Des Moines area. Later, the Sauk and Fox Indians
lived here. In 1843 the United States built a fort here to
keep peace between settlers and Indians. They called it
Fort Des Moines. Fort Des Moines grew into a town.
When Iowa was looking for a capital near the center of
the state, Des Moines people said, "Make it here!" But
other cities wanted to be the capital, too. The Des Moines
people won. In 1857 Des Moines became the capital.

The State Capitol building

Today, lawmakers from all over the Hawkeye State meet in the State Capitol building in Des Moines. The State Capitol sits on a hill. You can see the big golden dome from all around Des Moines.

Des Moines is Iowa's biggest manufacturing city. Farmers send fruits and vegetables to Des Moines. There they are put in cans and packages. Then they are sent all over the U.S. for people to eat. Tractors are made in Des Moines. Books and magazines are printed in Des Moines. Tools, tires, make-up, and medicine are four more products made here.

Above: The Des Moines Children's Zoo
Left: Drake University

Drake University is in Des Moines. A race called the Drake Relays brings runners from all over the U.S. to Drake each April. Drake is a very fine school.

The Des Moines Children's Zoo is just for children. There you can ride on a burro—or on an elephant. If you like science go to the Center of Science and Industry. You can see many famous paintings at the Des Moines Art Center.

Every August, the Iowa State Fair is held in Des Moines. At that time farmers bring in their best crops and animals to try to win the blue ribbon. They also learn about new farming methods.

Downtown Cedar Rapids

Cedar Rapids is in a hilly area of eastern Iowa. The first settler here was Osgood Shepard. He built a log cabin on the Cedar River in 1838. Later, farmers settled here because of the great farm land. The Sauk and Fox Indians who lived nearby were friendly to those first settlers.

The rivers, streams, and lakes in the area make Cedar Rapids a lovely city. The Cedar River flows right through the city. The river has very fast-moving water—called *rapids*—near the city. You can see how the city got its name.

Today ice cream, corn seed, animal feed, soft drinks, and breakfast cereals are made in Cedar Rapids. Trampolines are made here, too.

Waterloo is in northeastern Iowa. Waterloo was founded in 1845 by George and Mary Hanna and their family. They arrived here in covered wagons. According to one story, Mary Hanna named the town Waterloo.

Tractors are made in Waterloo. Tractors are used by farmers in Iowa and other states to pull farm machinery. Driving a tractor can be very dangerous work. You can visit the John Deere Waterloo Tractor Works. It is the largest tractor factory in the world. You'll see how they make tractors as safe as possible.

Bacon and hams are packed in Waterloo. Mail boxes and golf bags are made there.

Since 1910, the National Dairy Cattle Congress has been held in Waterloo in late September. People from all over the U.S. come to look at cattle and farm products here.

Julien Dubuque's grave

Remember Julien Dubuque, the lead miner who was Iowa's first settler? Dubuque sits next to the Mississippi River in northeastern Iowa. The city is located on seven hills. There is a monument to Julien Dubuque next to the Mississippi River, at the place where he is buried.

Today, food is packaged in Dubuque. Chemicals and furniture are also made there.

Crystal Lake Cave is near Dubuque. This cave was found by miners who were looking for lead. The cave has an underground lake inside it.

The Maquoketa (mah • qua • KEH • tah) Caves State Park is between Dubuque and Davenport. Here you can walk on trails that Indians used long ago. The caves are thought to have been the homes of Mound Builders.

Davenport is also on the Mississippi River, south of Dubuque. Davenport was named after George Davenport. He was a fur trader who helped found the town in 1836. Antoine LeClaire helped start the town, too. LeClaire also helped the great Indian chief, Black Hawk, write the story of his life.

The first railroad bridge to span the Mississippi River was completed at Davenport, in 1856. This bridge allowed thousands of people to come by train into Iowa.

Clothes, train equipment, cement, and metal are made in Davenport.

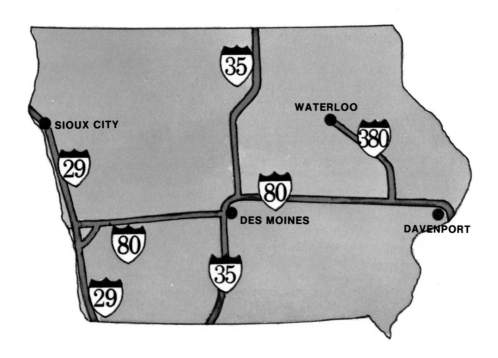

Sioux City is in western Iowa, next to the Missouri River. Both South Dakota and Nebraska are very near Sioux City. The city was named after the Sioux Indians who once lived in the area.

Lewis and Clark explored in this area in 1804. A nineteen-year-old man who was exploring with them died on the trip. His name was Charles Floyd. He was buried in Sioux City. The Floyd Monument honors him. It is 100 feet tall. The town of Sioux City was founded in 1854 by John Cook, who was exploring this region for the U.S. government.

Sioux City has one of the biggest popcorn plants in the U.S. It also has one of the biggest honey plants. And it has one of the largest plants for making dairy products.

Des Moines, Cedar Rapids, Davenport, Sioux City, Waterloo, and Dubuque are the six biggest cities in Iowa. Iowa has many smaller cities.

Iowa City was the capital of Iowa until 1857. The University of Iowa is there.

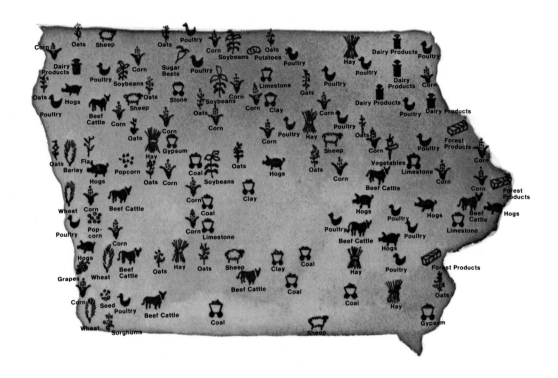

Ames is the home of the Iowa State University of Science and Technology. Many new farming methods are developed there.

Muscatine was named after the Mascoutin Indians. It is next to the Mississippi River.

Corn oil is made in Keokuk, named after Chief Keokuk. The writer Mark Twain once lived in Keokuk.

Council Bluffs is on the Missouri River. It was named for the cliffs next to the Missouri River. Grapes are grown in the area.

Washing machines are made in the city of Newton. Refrigerators and freezers are made at Amana. Amana was once a cooperative community where a religious group lived.

Cities and farms don't tell the whole story of the state. Iowa has had an interesting crop of people, too.

A U.S. president—Herbert Hoover—was born in West Branch, Iowa, on August 10, 1874. Early in life, Hoover ran a gold mine in Australia. He lived in many places of the world. He tried to help the poor people of the world after he was elected our 31st president in 1928. He also tried to help the American farmers.

William Cody was born in Le Claire, Iowa, in 1846, the year Iowa became a state. He was great at riding a horse. When Bill was a boy he rode for the Pony Express. The Pony Express delivered the mail in those days. He was also a great shot with a rifle. When a railroad was being built in Kansas, Bill Cody got food for

the workers by shooting buffalo. Once, Bill Cody had a
contest with another man to see who could shoot the
most buffalo. Bill Cody won. So he became known as
"Buffalo Bill." Buffalo Bill became an Indian scout and
an Indian fighter. Once Buffalo Bill had a fight to the
death with the Cheyenne (SHY • ann) Chief Yellow Hand.
Buffalo Bill won that fight. Later in life, Buffalo Bill
created his "Wild West Show." It had cowboys, Indians,
bucking broncos, and buffaloes. It showed what life was
like in the early days of the West.

The actor John Wayne was born in Winterset, Iowa, in
1907. Buffalo Bill probably would have liked John

HOOVER

CODY

WAYNE

Wayne. As a young man Wayne was a football player. Later he became a famous movie star. Most of his movies were Westerns. He starred in *Stagecoach, She Wore a Yellow Ribbon,* and *True Grit.*

Grant Wood was born in Anamosa in 1892. He became a famous painter. He painted pictures of Iowa farms. And he did paintings of Iowa farm people. Two of Grant Wood's famous works are "American Gothic" and "Young Corn." For a while Wood lived in Paris, France. But then he became homesick. So he returned to paint more pictures of the Hawkeye State. Wood is considered one of the great modern American artists. Grant Wood once ran an art colony in Stone City where other artists learned to paint.

Drake University relays are held each year in April.

Eight percent of America's food supply comes from Iowa.

Home to the Mound Builders . . . Herbert Hoover . . . Grant Wood . . . and John Wayne.

The land of the Ioway Indians . . . the Sioux . . . and the Sauk.

Great farmland where corn . . . soybeans . . . and hogs are raised.

The state with the most farmers.

This is Iowa—the Hawkeye State.

Facts About IOWA

Area—56,290 square miles (25th biggest state)

Greatest Distance North to South—210 miles

Greatest Distance East to West—324 miles

Border States—Minnesota on the north; Wisconsin and Illinois across the
Mississippi River on the east; Missouri to the south; Nebraska across the
Missouri River on the west; and South Dakota across the Big Sioux River on the
northwest

Highest Point—1,670 feet above sea level (in Osceola County)

Lowest Point—480 feet above sea level (where the Mississippi and Des Moines
rivers join in Lee County)

Hottest Recorded Temperature—118° (in Keokuk, on July 20, 1934)

Coldest Recorded Temperature—Minus 47° (in Washta, on January 12, 1912)

Statehood—Our 29th state, on December 28, 1846

Origin of Name Iowa—Named after the Ioway (also called the Iowa) Indians

Capital—Des Moines (1857)

Previous Capital—Iowa City

Counties—99

U.S. Senators—2

U.S. Representatives—6

Electoral Votes—8

State Senators—50

State Representatives—100

State Song—"Song of Iowa" by Samuel H.M. Byers

State Motto—*Our liberties we prize and our rights we will maintain.*

Nicknames—Hawkeye State, Corn State, Corn-Hog State, The Land Where the
Tall Corn Grows

State Seal—Adopted in 1847

State Flag—Adopted in 1921

State Flower—Wild rose

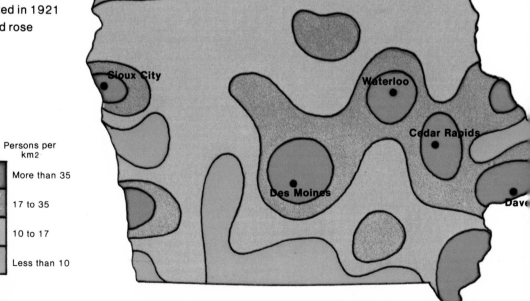

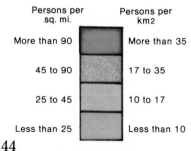

Persons per sq. mi.		Persons per km2
More than 90		More than 35
45 to 90		17 to 35
25 to 45		10 to 17
Less than 25		Less than 10

44

State Bird—Eastern goldfinch (wild canary)

State Tree—Oak

State Rock—Geode

Some Colleges and Universities—Coe College, Drake University, University of Dubuque, Grinnell College, University of Iowa, Iowa State University of Science and Technology, Upper Iowa University

Principal Rivers—Mississippi River, Missouri River, Big Sioux River

Some Other Rivers—Little Sioux, Raccoon, Des Moines, Skunk, Iowa, Cedar, Maquoketa

State Forests—6

State Parks—95

Animals—Gray foxes, red foxes, coyotes, raccoons, opossums, badgers, beavers, otters, woodchucks, bobcats, striped skunks, mink, whitetail deer, shrews, bats, squirrels, hummingbirds, whistling swans, wild turkeys, quail, pheasants, hawks, owls, ducks, geese, rattlesnakes, copperhead snakes, black snakes, fox snakes, milk snakes, bullsnakes

Fishing—Bass, trout, catfish, blue gill, northern pike, walleye, sturgeons, paddlefish, darters

Farm Products—Corn, soybeans, apples, onions, tomatoes, potatoes, cucumbers, hogs, beef cattle, dairy cattle, chickens, turkeys, eggs

Mining—Coal, gypsum, sand, gravel, clay, limestone, shale

Manufacturing Products—Food products, machinery, chemicals

Population—1980 census: 2,913,808 (1986 estimate: 2,851,000)

Major Cities

1980 Census

Des Moines 191,003
Cedar Rapids 110,243
Davenport 103,264
Sioux City   82,003
Waterloo   75,985
Dubuque   62,374

1984 Estimate

Des Moines 190,800
Cedar Rapids 108,700
Davenport 102,100
Sioux City 81,800
Waterloo 75,700
Dubuque 60,200

Iowa's History

Thousands of years ago the Mound Builders came to live in Iowa. They were related to the Indians who came later.

1673—Louis Joliet and Father Marquette explore Iowa for France

1682—La Salle claims large area of America, including Iowa, for France

1735—French fight Sauk and Fox Indians near where Des Moines is today

1762—Spain gains temporary control of large area, including Iowa

1788—Julien Dubuque settles near where Dubuque stands today

1799—Frenchman Louis Honore Tesson settles in Iowa

1800—France again controls Iowa

1803—United States buys Iowa and other lands from France

1804—Lewis and Clark go up Missouri River and explore Iowa shore; Charles Floyd dies on trip and is buried at Sioux City

1808—U.S. builds Fort Madison in Iowa

1812—Iowa is part of Territory of Missouri

1830—First school in Iowa begun by Dr. Isaac Galland near town of Galland

1832—Black Hawk loses Black Hawk War; according to Black Hawk Purchase, Indians give up strip of land in Iowa next to Mississippi River

1833—Towns of Dubuque, Burlington, and Fort Madison are founded

1834—Iowa becomes part of Territory of Michigan

1834—First church in Iowa is built at Dubuque

1836—Iowa becomes part of Territory of Wisconsin

1837—Sauk and Fox Indians give up their Iowa lands

1838—Iowa becomes part of Territory of Iowa

1843—Fort Des Moines built

1846—Iowa becomes our 29th state on December 28

1847—University of Iowa founded at Iowa City

1848—First telegraph built in Iowa

1851—First daily newspaper in Iowa is printed at Dubuque

1855—First railroad in Iowa

1856—First railroad bridge built across Mississippi River

1857—State constitution adopted that is still used today

1857—Sioux Indians kill 42 Iowans at Spirit Lake Massacre

1857—Des Moines becomes the capital of Iowa

1858—Iowa State Agricultural College (now Iowa State University of Science and Technology) founded at Ames

1861-65—Civil War; 80,000 Hawkeyes fight for North

1864—Famous Little Brown Church near Nashua is established

1874—Herbert Hoover is born at West Branch, Iowa, on August 10

1877—First telephone in Iowa

1912—Farm Bureau begun; helps teach farmers how to farm

1913—Keokuk Dam finished

1917—U.S. enters World War I; 113,000 Iowans fight

1928—Hawkeye Herbert Hoover is elected our 31st president

1941—U.S. enters World War II; 260,000 Iowa men and women in uniform

1946—Happy 100th birthday, Iowa!

1987—Terry E. Brandstad begins second term as governor

INDEX

47

About the Author:

Dennis Fradin attended Northwestern University on a creative writing scholarship and was graduated in 1967. While still at Northwestern, he published his first stories in *Ingenue* magazine and also won a prize in *Seventeen's* short story competition. A prolific writer, Dennis Fradin has been regularly publishing stories in such diverse places as *The Saturday Evening Post, Scholastic, National Humane Review, Midwest,* and *The Teaching Paper.* He has also scripted several educational films. Since 1970 he has taught second grade reading in a Chicago school—a rewarding job, which, the author says, "provides a captive audience on whom I test my children's stories." Married and the father of three children, Dennis Fradin spends his free time with his family or playing a myriad of sports and games with this childhood chums.

About the Artist:

Len Meents studied painting and drawing at Southern Illinois University and after graduation in 1969 he moved to Chicago. Mr. Meents works full time as a painter and illustrator. He and his wife and child currently make their home in LaGrange, Illinois.

Richard Wahl, graduate of the Art Center College of Design in Los Angeles, has illustrated a number of magazine articles and booklets. He is a skilled artist and photographer who advocates realistic interpretations of his subjects. He lives with his wife and two sons in Libertyville, Illinois.